A QUESTION OF EXISTENCE

MANYA J.

To all those who grieve too often, and to all those who are never able to do so.

Contents

Contents

Preface

This is really self indulgent I believe. These poems are all yours to read, but they're mine to tell.

There might be a pending question mark in the poem, in your mind even as you read on. That's good, that's the point. It is all very insubstantial, there are a lot of concepts questioned, defined, thought over, defended and even eye rolled at with words. Even still, all is meant to be not limited to that. A lot of hatred and anger you will find prominent here, so, I guess be ready? Just kidding. Not.

In all honesty I question my own self in here more than anything.

It's quite a pretty word isn't it? 'Poetry'. However pretty the words sound, they're all just a little too sad, just a little to embellished, just a little too dragged out and exaggerated. Some of what is on here is quite real and has infact occured and is quite questionable which sounds like it should be the point, when you read the title right? But the rest are more surreal, and very much fiction. All I can say is, have a strong heart, have some tissues at the ready if you plan on reading these in one go, and just let the poetry take you along where you feel it's headed. Do not look for my guidance or me in any way or form. This is your copy and is to be read and understood by you. Otherwise this copy of this book wouldn't be in your hand, and I wouldn't be setting these poems free from my mind and heart.

These poems more or less are for people in high school or older, since there are some gore and alot of traumatic themes. Please don't let these land in the hands of a child. I do not wish to be the cause of any crying children.

Acknowledgements

"Write hard and clear about what hurts." ~Ernest Hemingway. I may not be a fan of Hemingway as a person, but these words, did in fact allow me to continue writing about all the bad memories that keep nagging me. The memories which always make me question a lot of things. And also, this particular quote made me worry less about if my poems were too sad. Because that is something I should least worry about, these are *my* poems, about *my* experiences.

The fourth poem in this manuscript though, is whole heartedly dedicated to someone who is always there for me, I wrote it for them as a birthday present and I mean every word of it.

I would also like to mention here another friend of mine, Anoushka Joshi, who has been there to read everything I wrote, since the day I started writing and still does. She is I could say one of the biggest enthusiasts of whatever I write, the response I always get whenever I say I have something for her to read genuinely makes me so happy and motivated to share my writing. She is my beta reader, and the one to have a front row seat to all my first and last drafts.

1. To Vivaan,

There used to be pictures of him in our home
There used to be talk of him inspired by those pictures
Now, there's this silence that hangs over stories of him
Now, there's this emptiness where there used to be him
The seven-year-old boy who was dead in my arms
A brother, a memory, and a quiet thought that makes me cry
is he
Laughter was he, joy was he, neglecting him is the guilt that is
me
Always on his priority was me, always trying the best to
appease me was he
It has been now over seven years, it aches me to know
That I have known him for the same amount of time that I
have lost him
It reminds me, that I couldn't weep in his name for half a
decade
It reminds me how my chest always aches at the mention of
his name
It reminds me of the secrets we shared that no longer in my
memory remain
It reminds me of how I am feeling his face in my evocation
starting to fade
Which in turn brings me back to how,

There used to be pictures of him in our house.

• 2 •

2. Yearn

All I ever do is yearn
Yearn for passion suffocating and bright
Yearn for people not mine
Yearn for an existence without fright
Yearn to stop the thoughts that kill me inside
Yearn to receive the fruit for all the good I actually tried
Yearn for a world without lie
Yearn to truly defy
Yearn for darkness in a room full of light
Yearn for all I encounter to drop dead aside
Yearn to discover and find
A place to call home
A place to cover my face and hide
As I scream and wail
And feel my breath as it begins to fail
Imprisoned and frail
In presence of the one considered divine
Begging on knees
As they begin to decay
Clutching my head in hopeless anguish
And a grappling feel of dismay
Shrieking in pain
Face streaked with tears

Asking for it to cease

Weeping that knows no limit, pleading for release

From the curse

The curse that made me

Yearn and yearn and yearn

Each day pathetic

Each day inane

Each day bringing a loss of the sane

Loss which brings a world greying

Closer to its calamity

I look back at my words in pity

For I realize I am not alone entrapped

This unyielding curse which proves itself an inescapable fact

Since we yearn from the very first breath

Till we reach our inevitable yet liberating death

All anyone truly does is yearn

3. Within You

Imagine if someone pulled out all the poetry in you, turned it into ink, and handed you a quill. And as you dip that very quill into that very ink, all that was ever beautiful inside you is now laid out all too perfectly still beside you, as you stare at it and contemplate whatever must now be left within you.

4. To Kanak,

Right at the cusp of Spring, you came forth in my life

At the birthday of a friend, where I met my own self but older and more nice

The rare occurrence of such a rapport wasn't one known to me till that night

A being so sublime as you, a figure of comfort and solace

The existence of caliber such as yours, that too, to have as a friend still shocks me today

In your presence I'm reminded of, sunlight and cats, my very own safe space

Never do I consider myself of better luck than the time we spend together

Creating art, engaging in our favorite game, watching films, or just conversing at leisure

Those I whole heartedly believe are some of my most content memories ever

You've gone through more than enough hurt for a lifetime, still enduring the bilge of people

you are the most expressive person I know in spite of it all, with still cunning treacle

you inspire me, the one person with whom I am most alike, we are as if one another's sequel.

5. Rainbow

From blue to yellow
From yellow to red
The gradient glows
After the rain has left
And the sun has shown
The purple at the edge
Bi product of red to blue
Out of touch with red it is alleged
The one last in queue
With half itself at the other end
Silly little thoughts in my head
Of the vibrant colors in the sky
With their brilliant bend
Which manage to catch the eye
A phenomenon which transcends

6. The Betrayal of Words

The words I wrote at night were moonlit with meaning, passion, and a charming darkness but, as the light came so did the sun and my words then decided to betray me. They became bright, they burned my eyes, they no longer held the meaning that had come out of my soul, I cannot face them with the same emotion I felt before. And when I look at them in that light, a little part of me dies every time.

7. At The Art Gallery

Their each step restrained yet eager.
Their head brimming with misty thoughts.
Their vision clouded with admiration.
Strolling on through the quiet, deserted walkway.
Surrounded by emotion, longing, and secrets.
All hidden behind those breathtaking canvases,
And brooding sculptures.

8. Stars Held Dear

Staring at the stars, I breath in tranquility through tainted air, I smile at the moon, the only one allowed to witness it in its true essence, I let the brain dissipate from my body as I at last find freedom from myself and the gravity of all my thoughts and troubles as I feel them adagio amount to nothing; my eyes remain glued to the dark sky until they become heavy and drift back into draining thoughts, but I don't fret for a moment, because I know the stars that I hold so dear, above me they will once again appear.

9. A Person Too Real

Hysterically real, I set my gaze on this person
They remind me to be heedful of what I utter
Poignant in every aspect of the word
So visible, and determined to be more
So raucous and unafraid to be so
So unflappable and unbothered they seem
A person who causes a dispute within me
Are they someone I too wish to become?
Or someone I should abhor the very being of?

10. In A Flash

Flesh raw and new
Weak and vulnerably fresh
Introduced to the morning dew
But even before the first stretch
The skin drained of its hue
Already branded with the first etch
Burning now, lips now being sew
Watch it as it's torn to shreds
Watch as they approach it with forks and spoons
The beasts who feast away at all that's left

11. Ensnared Among Their Voices

Enwreathed in the cacophonous blare
That all these people cause, have me ensnared
Distorted conversations, none ever comprised of me
Though quite impeding they prove to be
Obstructing every thought, not an ounce of privacy
It is quite the atrocious irony
Since, nevertheless I'm always left completely alone
Stranded in the middle of all this noise, chilled to the bone
Barriers that I created to shut it all off
I can't take it anymore, it just proves to be for naught
I find myself plead to make it stop
But it does so never
Instead, it continues to grow louder ever
As I continue to shrivel myself and struggle to hide
The pages that I used to read, and used to write
Don't seem to make do anymore
The sole lit screen in the darkened room
Doesn't quite do the ol' trick anymore
The voices have made their way into my head
They reside there
They implore and contaminate my being
I am hence corrupted

I remain sitting here in my perpetuate silence
Puzzled and paralyzed as if in a strict compliance
Enveloped in this raucous din
The one created by the ol' torturous mind within
Featuring the tumult of those around
Those whose voices keep me forever bound
Those who I fear never will
Cease until I am at last killed

12. Embody Knowledge

I want every poem ever written to be carved in my mind,

I want to know every word from every language in existence,

I want to know of every empire ever fallen,

I want to know all that history knows,

I want to read every story that could make one cry,

I want the ability to play any instrument I see,

I want to know everything about the stars

I want to know all that's known and all that's unknown

I love being in knowledge,

I love the feeling of knowing

I'd rather know and submit to madness than

Neglect and remain in the so called "bliss" of ignorance

I wish to embody all that can be known

I wish to embody knowledge in its literal sense

13. About Cutting

The grip at my throat
Keeps getting harder to control
Eyes brimming with tears not in flow
Ears filled with a heartbeat of their own
As my limbs grow cold
And my face goes warm in a color quite bold
I feel my conscious start to float
As I refuse to release the breath I continue to hold

I will not let them out
All the tears and obscenities I wish to shout
Sighing in defeat, as my breath comes out in doubt
I sense the knife I had thoughtlessly grabbed
Now being gripped with frightening force in my hand
I don't hesitate, even as my heart against my chest bangs
The sight of my own blood drives me mad
Anything but to be seen being vulnerable
The cuts may leave scars on my body inseparable
And it may not be pleasurable
But alas! I say at least it's blood instead of held off tears
No one shall every witness my grief or my fears
Even after I eventually wither along the years

14. Losing A Soul

Dragged through the dirt
Into oblivion my soul is thrust
As my body is left to gather dust
With cotton my body I try to stuff
A plaything is just what I've become
I let me wither from a single touch
I lost favor with the world, and it hurts
My blood has had enough
The other side for me no longer works
Physically I remain here stuck
Driving myself insane in my skull

15. Frankenstein From Scratch

I create my own monster from scratch

This giant beast that I piece and attach

Each component made intricately to be bound together

With one another, each piece is as light as a feather

The whole lot meant to be placed by hand, to be stitched and stacked

A Frankenstein of my own that I create right from scratch

I make sure to not give it eyes, for it shouldn't suffer

From the harsh and brutal sights out in the world, a life crusher

I make sure to not give it ears, for I couldn't let it bear

The abominably abysmal and scarring sounds we hear

I make sure to not give it a mind, for I would never want it be caught

Up in the pain of having its own unbearable and ultimately anguishing thought

I make sure to give it a heart, since without an opponent

A heart in a body without a brain sounds unimaginably pleasant

I make sure to give it a mouth but stitch it shut

So that it represents it's painlessness without any words or such

A Frankenstein of mine, neither eyed nor eared
A Frankenstein of mine, unminded with a heart and lips sealed
A monster by name this creature I lifed and lightly pieced
Face a mess of nothing, it's exterior is bulky to be appeared
A most beloved monster that I keep by my side
A monster now complete and to keep it is mine

16. Just An Idea

Ideas cannot kill you
Dreaming will not harm you
Airy hopes even just a few
Let the thoughts stay with you
Even if just for a moment or two
Acting on each and every thought
Is anyways possible not
So, why not just let yourself be lost
Just for an instant short
Without letting people tie you in knots

17. Anger? No, Grief.

If my anger was grief all along
Will my grief introduce itself
As anger due time? Or is it to stay?
The latter sounds petrifying
But is also the one which rings true
Why? I wonder quite intensely
Anger has always been a fuel
To my regular emotion, I can not
Fathom it simply just having been
Something entirely else all this time
It makes me ponder upon all I've ever felt
Have my own feelings been tricking me?
Did anything I ever feel even exist at all?

18. On My Wall

Writing quotes on my wall, so
When I most need to hear them
I can simply read them whenever I want
Somehow, I find it strange though
That a wall full of quotes,
From people who do not exist,
And from people I have never met
Can make me misty and provide
Comfort to me when nobody else could.
So, I add on to it, with words of my own
Which makes it seem stranger still
To see my own voice mixed with
All these people whose words I admire
I added drawings of mine and of others
I added pictures of the stars
I added phases of the moon
It now looks so complete,
Oh! My wall, a most
Precious sight to me

19. Lifeless Eyes

I find there to be a certain horrifying fascination in lifeless eyes
The bare transfixed gaze out into nothingness
Overcome with eternal tenebrosity, not an ounce of light in
there
Completely empty, completely dull, and oh so wispy
They might appear frightening to eyes of soul and mind
Oh, but how do eyes alive not see the contrasting beauty in
the eyes dead
The way they no longer contain anything beyond them
Except just a brain oh, so free of thought
Except just a heart oh, so still
Except just blood oh, so cold
The eyes that are vacant of life
The mortality so visible and clear, oh
The divinity of those eyes

20. Cosmos

Infinite space they say
Infinite the only word they believe fits
But is it even nearly enough?
To describe this existing continuum?
So vast
So free
So unknowable
So out of reach
How can it be that a single word
Be enough to cover even just a tenth of it?
Yet how many words would be
Enough to cover it? An infinite? To assume
Not being cognizant of the cosmos
Even in the slightest is
So unfair, so unjust, oh so inequitable
It truly is frustrating
Everything of it known so far
Seems so trifling in its comparison
To reside in the cosmos, but alas,
Only manage to live in its theories

21. When 'It' Hits

As I sit with myself in the dark
As music resonates in my ears
As my vision sulks the ceiling
My thoughts at lightspeed
Searching through the cold
Their pace melting the ice
Opening the wrong gates
Peeking behind the disguise
They show me these fragments
Unknown which seem to be
Known they may be, though
They pose their cause futile
Even still I examine them
I turn them in my hands
And then with no reprimand
They gash at my eyes
They spike at my heart
And pierce through my memory
Tethering its pieces without consent
To the inexplicable conscious
Of emotions pull at me
All they leave behind is
The throb at my head

The ache in my chest
And the salt on my face

22. Lost To Time

Today, I declare myself a cause lost to time,
One lost on meaning or sanity,
As my head calls for my death opined
It craves death oh so violently,
That without having it enshrined
It'll wish it upon merely anyone in sight
Whoever it declares has it defied
Creating an aura radiating daggers of despise,
As that aura sits on me like heavy fog,
With its most suffocating bind,
One oh so tight in tight in its grip,
That it erases everything else inside,
As it creates unfathomably horrid scenes
In my mind, such vivid scenes of a slayer,
A killer determined to destruct blind
The day I saw the eyes,
It broke me as I discovered they were mine,
My head had gone white by that time,
As I came back, mentally flooded at night
So much so, as I had barely recognized
The taste of copper at my lip by an unintended bite.

23. More Than Noise

There's noise
I'm sure there is
I can hear it
It is sound
And it vibrates
I can feel it
My soles can,
And so can my palms
The beat is loud
It thumps in my chest
Even if it is so
Evident in its existence
Why does it feel
So quiet right now?
Why does my head
Experience this
Strange, unnerving calm?
Well. In the end
It's just noise
Not spoken words
That must be it
That must be why
Why it is different.

24. A Dance for The Ghosts

"Beware of the ghosts!" I hear

As I stride across the wild

Multiple voices whisper warnings

I stare in awe as the trees begin to clear

The wind picks up and blows off my ragged hide

Crows caw aloud and fly away flapping their wings

An age-old castle covered in moss seems to have appeared

In ruins but intact still the same, I let my instinct be my guide

Walking in, my ears are graced by music that of violins

I walk in, and come across a light to my side as I sheer

Turning towards a ballroom well lit, with not a soul in sight

Still dark outside I notice through a glass with a small skull at its windowsill

Going in the high ceiling hall, poetry along with the music I now hear

Is it strange that I do not shiver in fear or attempt to flight?

I do now realize the presence of the ghosts awarned in the hills

With no purpose or task left I dance underneath the chandelier

The ghosts do not take me prey, as they continue their song for the night.

25. The Concept of Bleeding

Why is bleeding such a sad occasion?

Why do we romanticize it still?

Is it because what's inside comes out by force?

Was it ever meant to witness such a world?

The world outside, which draws out the red from within...

Whether it was a cut of choice, it was still a cut that was made

The red never comes out at its own will

It may be natural to bleed from below

But elsewhere you won't bleed unless too harshly poked

Blood is meant to stay inside and do its work

It was never meant to come out and play

Because in the end, it would be simply washed away

The red is gone now.

Only a scar left behind now

Only its sting left behind now.

26. My Life as A Book?

• 31 •

What if my whole life
Was a story in play
An unknown book
By an unknown author
That you'd find
In an old bookstore
I would imagine it to be
The kind of book that
Takes your breath away
Refusing to give it back
Until you're choking
Choking on your own tears
Before your breath finds you
You look back at the book
You had failed to realize that
The page was now wet
The book was now over

27. Fire

Fire, a substance to be controlled
One, which spreads only when there exist entities to burn
It's understood to only be controlled
By man, and it's kind in turn
Even still, if in a situation untold
Fire, will bring about chaos in return
Bright, unpredictable yet restrainable, oh! Behold!
This creature unlike another
A form of life on its own!
Conquering the air we breathe for itself with gern
Marking its death with soot and the ash of all it killed alone
Flame, which exists beyond what we learn
Beyond our reach in the stars that shine atop.

28. Numb

The faint feeling of my fingers turning blue, going numb from the cold, as it spreads along my body. Numb, is it a feeling? Or the lack of such? Is it the sensation in your body at the ache of exhaustion? Tired, tired of the cold, tired of reason, tired of your limbs, tired of touch, tired of perceiving, tired of being? Extreme, extreme exhaustion, does it bring about this suppression that we name numb? The body continues to work, it's just the feel which seems to fade and give out. A paralysis of feeling.

29. A Wish to Weep

Going back home,
Sitting by myself on the bus
With this ache in my eyes
And a wish in my heart
Denied by my brain
Held off by restrain
A silent urge to weep
An urge that I am sad to say
I feel too often these days
Misery of past memories
As well as new ways I find
To give myself pain
Cause this continuous ache
The one in my eyes
That I experience everyday

30. Grey

The sky aged with the night
The water fell with me
Looking up I don't believe
It's silver, it's all grey
It's always been grey
Even when it's blue or black
Grey is the state of grief
Whether in the sky or in me
Grey is all I seem to see